CONSTRUCTING YOUR BUSINESS
A BLUEPRINT FOR SUCCESS

Your Formula for a Successful Business
Starting from the Ground Up

Designed for those starting a small business with a focus on
Consultants, Counselors, Psychologists, Complementary and
Alternative Medicine and Holistic Nursing

BY
M. Ron Eslinger, CAPT USN Retired
RN, CRNA, MA, APN, BCH, FNCH

1

Money never starts an idea; it is the idea that starts the money.
William J Cameron

CONSTRUCTING YOUR BUSINESS
A BLUEPRINT FOR SUCCESS

Your Formula
For a Successful Business
Starting from the Ground Up

Designed for those starting a small business with a focus on Consultants, Counselors, Psychologists, Complementary and Alternative Medicine, and Holistic Nursing

M. Ron Eslinger
CAPT USN Retired
RN, CRNA, MA, APN, BCH, FNGH

Published by
Healthy Visions Publishing an imprint of the Healthy Visions
351 Market Street, Clinton, TN 37716

Editing by Shade Powell

Printed in the United States of America.

Acknowledgments

I am indebted to those who read the manuscript and provided me with the benefit of their thinking regarding the usefulness of this book. I started my first business as a freelance Nurse Anesthetist in 1974. I did so with absolutely no knowledge or preconceived notions of doing more than going to the hospital or physician that had hired me for that day, giving anesthesia and collecting my pay. That style of doing business was great until tax time. I had made a few mistakes.

That is why in 1979 when I opened my hypnosis practice, I knew enough to hire an accountant. I ran that business part-time from 1979 to 1985. I learned a lot about what I would have done differently. Unfortunately, what I would have done differently should have been done before I started the business, not after I closed it. My main regret was that I did not know about the number of resources available to those wanting to start a small business.

In 1999 I started Healthy Visions as a nurse continuing education program specializing in training nurses in hypnosis. I retired from the Navy in 2003 and opened the Healthy Visions Wellness Center. What I am sharing in this book are the lessons I learned about Business.

Dedicated to My Wife, Karen

This book is dedicated to my wife, Karen, who stood by me during all my dreams and ideas of having my own business and being my own boss. She was my cheerleader during the frustrations, fears, anxieties, and failures that accompany any business success.

Foreword

Ron Eslinger is a retired Navy Captain and owner and CEO of Healthy Visions, Sedation Certification, founder of the American Association of Moderate Sedation Nurses (AAMSN), MyCEcredit, and the American School for Clinical Hypnosis, International (ASCHI). He graduated from St. Mary's School of Nursing, Knoxville, TN, in 1970 and completed Nurse Anesthesia training at the University of Tennessee in 1974. He received his BS degree in Professional Arts from Saint Joseph's College in Wenham, Maine, 1990, and his master's degree in Foreign Affairs for National Defense and Strategic Studies from the United States Naval War College, Newport, RI in 1994.

In 1979 I had no thought or intent to be in business for myself. However, a simple comment from my wife set me on a path that included the start-up of multiple businesses. Four of those I started while working as a CRNA and another while an officer in the Navy. Every business I started is still in effect today with a couple under different names. I compiled this book in 2006 from my experiences and lack of experience to help others.

A quick list of start-ups:
1. 1979 - Knoxville Center for Clinical Hypnosis
2. 1982 – CRNA, Continuing Education Seminars
3. 1984 – Developed subliminal tapes with biorhythmic music for anesthesia patients
4. 1999 – Became a Certified Instructor for the National Guild of Hypnotists, which continues today.
5. 2001 – Created Healthy Visions Hypnosis with online products.
6. 2004 – Retired from the Navy, opened an office and expanded government contracting and corporate training.
7. 2006 – Expanded to non-anesthesia nurse sedation training.
8. 2008 – Founded the American Association of Moderate Sedation Nurses
9. 2004-2020 Healthy Visions has exploded into many areas of live and online training.

Table of Contents

"He who has not first laid his foundations may be able with great ability to lay them afterward, but they will be laid with trouble to the architect and danger to the building."

Niccolo Machiavelli, *The Prince* Italian *dramatist, historian, & philosopher (1469 - 1527)*

Like building a home, a business needs a strong and sturdy foundation. In the business world, the foundation is the business owner. Many entrepreneurs start out thinking that because they love what they do and are proficient in their industry, that they will make a successful business owner. That is partly true. But that is just the beginning.

Some professionals think that if they owned their own business, they'd make more money, have more freedom for creativity, more control over situations, and more security with regards to staying employed. There are many factors to consider when deciding to open your own business. The risk of losing money and personal assets, working longer hours than they initially thought necessary, the pressure to keep the business profitable, lack of a steady paycheck, abiding by governmental laws and regulations, and the tremendous amount of stress that comes with a new venture.

Should you be a business owner?

Being honest about why you want to start a business is the first step. When you answer that question, you can ask yourself if you have what it takes to become a business owner.

How do you rate yourself with the following questions?

With 1 being needs improvement, 5 being average and 10 being superior, circle the number that applies to your skills, abilities, and attitudes.

1. **Confidence** – belief in your business and the future success it will bring
   1 2 3 4 5 6 7 8 9 10

2. **Decision Maker** – being able to analyze situations and make the proper choices

   1 2 3 4 5 6 7 8 9 10

3. **Communicate** – being able to express your desires to others
   1 2 3 4 5 6 7 8 9 10

4. **Expertise** – technical ability to continue growing your business
   1 2 3 4 5 6 7 8 9 10

5. **Risktaker** – investing time, money, effort and energy to accomplish your goals

   1 2 3 4 5 6 7 8 9 10

6. **Inspiration** – being able to work with others and grow their loyalty
   1 2 3 4 5 6 7 8 9 10

7. **Motivation** – mental and physical drive to accomplish your goals
   1 2 3 4 5 6 7 8 9 10

If you feel that you honestly possess all seven traits necessary to enter the business ownership world, you are on your way. However, if you feel that an area or two needs work, ask yourself what you can do to improve on those issues. If communication is not your strong point, look to join an organization like Toast Masters. If you feel you need more technical ability, consider taking a class at the local college or university, or sign up for additional continuing education classes offered through various organizations.

By taking action now on possible shortcomings, you'll be able to withstand the pressure and have more confidence as you continue on your way to starting and building your business.

There have been numerous studies on what it takes to be a successful business owner. One's character and behaviors are important factors to consider when starting a business.

Answer the following questions honestly about your personality traits.

- ✓ Do you have good health?
- ✓ Are you a self-starter?
- ✓ Are you responsible?
- ✓ Are you a leader?
- ✓ Can you make tough decisions?
- ✓ Are you organized?
- ✓ Are you a leader?
- ✓ Do you like people in general?
- ✓ Do you finish what you start?
- ✓ Are you a hard worker?
- ✓ Can you work smart?

Again, if you find there are areas within your character that need improvement, you must find ways to bring about a change. Or, if, for example you aren't very organized, you can hire staff to make up for your deficit. However, when starting a new business, money is always an issue. Check out your local library for books on organization or talk to another person who you admire that has organizational skills.

As you can see, the first step is usually the toughest part of starting a business. Being honest and open about your strengths and weaknesses can seem a bit daunting, but as you build your foundation upon truthful evaluation, your business will be able to grow and prosper.

Market Research

You have now assessed your strengths and weaknesses in regard to becoming a business owner. The second step is to determine if your service is needed in the community. Most new business owners decide to build their business in their back yard. Prevent a possible disaster by researching the need for your service within your community prior to start-up.

There is a vast amount of interest and information related to the Complementary Care industry on a national level. It will be up to you to research if your community fits the average profile of a complementary care client. The following are four areas that you need to address to see if your service will fill a community need.

- Community Population – basic demographics are usually available at the local Chamber of Commerce.

- Competition — Easy to Google, search Chamber of Commerce directory and newspapers. If there is an established hypnotist/hypnotherapist, make an appointment. Visit their office, read their literature, review their price schedules, check their website.

- Business Restrictions — check out the city/county business office for licensing, zoning, permitting requirements.

- Community Need — mail or telephone surveys can help determine whether your service will fill a need in the community.

Once you gather the data from the various sources, ask yourself the following questions.

- Who is my typical client?
- What percent of the population fits my client profile?
- What is the community's average income?
- Is the income level enough to support complementary care expenses?
- Is the community's population growing?
- Are new businesses being established?
- If there is another business, what will my niche be?

By asking these questions upfront, you can then determine whether this community will be able to support your business. If not, check into the surrounding areas. Is there a larger community nearby? Is it worth the commute to locate there?

Part-Time or Full Time

If you currently have a full-time career, the best situation is to stay with that paycheck until such time that your business needs more of your time. Of course, if you have enough funds in the bank to support going full-time at the beginning, that is the ideal. Being able to give your full attention to the start-up, marketing, networking, and advancement of your business keeps the momentum flowing and gives your clients the impression of a total commitment from you. The perception of success will increase client confidence.

Partners

Another approach to consider is having a partnership. Therapy as a complementary care industry, can work well with massage therapy, acupuncture, reiki, to name just a few.

Some benefits of partnering are:

- Reduce personal risk
- Additional funds
- Emotional support
- Share management demands
- Increase services provided

But if considering a partner, every issue, from financial to emotional, needs to be discussed, agreed upon, and put in writing. Nothing is more difficult than to divorce a partner in the business world.

Business Structure

Whether you start your practice individually or with a partner, the business structure needs to be researched to fit your personal and financial needs best.

Things to consider are:

1. How will I track my income?
2. Will I have employees?
3. What share of personal risk am I willing to take?
4. What type of business do I want?

Some of the forms of business are sole proprietorship, partnership, corporation, Limited Liability Company, and limited partnership. In general terms, a Sole Proprietorship means that all income generated for the business is passed to the owner. You may have a partner and structure as a sole proprietor as each partner would then share in the profits.

Generally, a Doing Business As (DBA) is all that's needed to establish this form of structure.

A **Corporation** separates the business from your obligations. In a corporation, you will then be considered an employee. One of the main advantages of forming a corporation is it may shield you in the face of a lawsuit. However, you, as an individual, may still be named. The paperwork required to form a corporation and the tax pros and cons is different in each state. Seeking the advice of your attorney and/or CPA can save you time and money in the long run.

In the middle is a **Limited Liability Company**. Generally, there is one person who is in control of the company in a day to day capacity. This person is also liable for the actions of the business. The partner has a limited amount of control and therefore limited liability as well. The best way to decide on your business structure is to be advised by your attorney and/or accountant. But remember, you may also change your structure as your business grows and becomes more profitable.

Licenses and Permits

Just as building a house foundation needs licensing and permits, so does building a business. Therapy is a service. And most services require a business license. Licensing requirements vary from state to state as well as city and county. Most areas charge a nominal fee for a business license. While others also collect a portion of the business profits. If your business is located within the city limits, some areas require a county license as well, so make sure to check with both agencies.

Call your city business licensing authority. Check the requirements needed and if they have a website to download the application. Knowing the requirements will save valuable time in your start-up process. Applications are then generally sent to the zoning department or city planning department to make sure the business location meets the code guidelines. Therefore, it's a good idea to have your business location chosen. This is true for a home-based business as well.

State licensing for therapy varies from state to state. Check via the internet about your state requirements and registering your business.

If your business plans on selling products, you'll need to obtain a seller's permit or sales tax permit. Check with your state as to how to get this permit. By having a sales tax number, you will forgo paying taxes on items purchased from wholesalers. However, sales tax will then need to be collected, reported, and remitted to the state.

Permits are generally required for yard signage. Ordinances usually restrict the size, location, lighting, and structure. If renting a space, check with your landlord as well. Any agreement with the property owner should be approved in writing with a copy of the sign.

To have a successful business, you must be operating legitimately. Licenses and permits are to safeguard the consumer, as well as give credibility to the business. The amount of time required to be properly authorized to conduct business is well worth the effort.

Blueprints

Complete the following checklist to see if you need further research or improvements before continuing your business building.

Have you had any business training?
    Yes   No
Are you the entrepreneurial type?
    Yes   No
Are you willing to risk time and money?
    Yes   No
Have you researched your business start-up?
    Yes   No
Is your family supportive of your business plans?
    Yes   No
Have you researched your area's market?
    Yes   No

Is there a need for your service?

     Yes   No

Will your business have competition?

     Yes   No

Have you visited your competition?

     Yes   No

Can you start your business while remaining employed?

     Yes   No

Do you know the benefits of each type of structure?

     Yes   No

Do you know which business structure to use?

     Yes   No

Do you want and/or need a partner?

     Yes   No

Have you considered a possible person as a partner?

     Yes   No

Have you contacted your area's business department?

     Yes   No

Do you know what license(s) and/or permit(s) you'll need?

     Yes   No

If home-based, have you contacted the zoning department?

     Yes   No

Is your business location properly zoned?

     Yes   No

Websites of interest

U.S. Small Business Administration
www.sba.gov

Entrepreneur Assist
www.entrepreneur.com

Ewing Marion Kauffman Foundation for Entrepreneurs
www.kauffman.org

"Obstacles are what you see when you take your eyes off the goal."

Unknown-

Just as important as constructing a solid foundation on which to build, the framing of your business needs to be solid, able to support growth, and weather economic climate changes. Setting goals and drafting a plan is the framework of your business.

Goal Setting

Goals and goal setting are integral parts of each aspect of your business startup. You were asked questions in Chapter One to help you determine if you are prepared to start a business and know the type of business you are considering. There are six aspects of goal setting listed to help you develop a business plan based on:

1. Your buy-in

2. Your expected reward

3. How you imagine yourself in business

4. How you think others see your business

5. How you overcome obstacles and temptations

6. Success

Your buy-in

1. Do you believe in you? What does your business plan reveal about your commitment to you and your business? Are your self-esteem, dedication, and preparation above average? Average in these areas is a sure prescription for failure. 85% of small businesses fail. Most businesses fail because of inadequate attention to the principles in Chapter One. Make a list of your traits positive and negative.

Stop Thinking in terms of limitations and start thinking in terms of possibilities.
Terry Josephson

Your reward

2. What is it that motivates you? Is it money, recognition, awards, helping others, and being your own boss? Does your business plan blueprint your intentions and expectations? Write down your mile markers to your goal and prioritize them.

Self-image sets the boundaries of individual accomplishments.
Maxwell Maltz

Imagine yourself in business

3. Can you imagine, visualize and pretend that you have accomplished your goal. You are opening the door to your own business. It can be counseling, coaching, complementary

or alternative therapies? Take time out daily to imagine yourself completing the things you need to complete to open the door to your business.

All of our dreams can come true, if we have the courage to pursue them.

Walt Disney

How others see your business

4. You have opened your practice. Do you understand *The Secret* to attracting clients? Do you have a vision board (putting pictures on a board of that which you want to accomplish)? Can you vividly imagine with passion, your business growing? When you do, you will be successful. I recommend the book or video *The Secret*.

Man can only receive what he sees himself receiving.

Florence Scovel Schinn

Obstacles and temptations

5.   What obstacles and temptations are you ready to overcome? When this question was asked to a group, one person responded that he was addicted to watching television every night. He set his first goal and reached it. He committed to using his TV time to develop and implement his business plan. Like most who take 6-12 months to open their business, he opened the first phase of his business in seven months. Two weeks earlier than his calendar date. It is a booming business today. He identified his obstacle and used it to his benefit?

I will ignore the voice that tells me I cannot. I will listen to the voice which says I CAN.

Jay Scott

Success

6. Reaching your goals. Follow the concepts of this book, and you will accomplish your goals. But first, you must have realistic goals that are written down (your business plan) and visualized daily.

"Whatever the mind of man can conceive and believe it can achieve."

Napoleon Hill

Once you understand the six concepts of goal setting, you are ready to draft your business plan to ensure that you have control of your business. Your goals and business plan allow you to build safely rather than haphazardly. By putting your ideas and goals on paper, you'll have to think through possible problems and resolve them with foresight. Drafting a business plan is an exercise of addressing any potential pitfalls, estimating costs and profits, developing a marketing strategy, and planning for growth. Any problems that arise can be researched and restructured before opening day.

Many new business owners get stuck at this point. They believe that a business plan is only necessary if you're trying to secure a loan. However, having written goals and a plan to achieve them allows possible mistakes to take place on paper, without being costly.

The first step is to ask the following goal-oriented questions:

1. Why do I want to be a business owner?

2. How much money do I want to make annually?

3. When do I need to make a profit?

4. What will owning a business help me to attain?

5. Are there any areas in my life I don't want the business to interfere with?

6. Do I want to have employees?

7. Do I want to expand and grow my business?

8. What are my aspirations?

The Business Plan

Now that you have your goals, the second step is to draft a plan to realize your goals. There are hundreds of books based solely on the topic of writing a business plan. Whether you are writing a plan to secure a start-up loan or to just have an outline of your business and growth, the time it takes to write the plan is well worth the effort.

The main components of a business plan

✓ Cover Page

✓ Table of Contents

✓ Executive Summary

✓ Business Description

✓ Service Description

✓ Competitive Analysis

✓ Marketing Plan

✓ Operations Plan

✓ Financial Plan

✓ Appendix

Each section of the business plan should help clarify your goals. Keep your writing detailed and specific. Your plan is not a novel, so the prose is not necessary. The basic outline is logical and progressive to show a step by step guide on how you intend to start, run, and grow your business.

Set aside some time daily to complete a small section of your plan. Keep in mind that the business plan is a tool to help you keep and maintain control over your business. Start by just completing each section by writing down your ideas and goals. Editing, researching data, and proofing can be done after your draft.

Cover Page

Essential information needed on the cover page is:
1. Name of the business
2. Address
3. Phone, fax, email
4. Name of owner

The cover page should be precise and neat. Do not clutter it with large typeface or huge graphics. If you have a logo, place it on the cover page.

Table of Contents

Again, the purpose here is to make finding information easy for your reader. Keep it simple by staying in the same format as your outline and placing a page number in each section. Using subheadings can be overwhelming. Use subheadings sparingly if at all.

Executive Summary

The executive summary is an essential section of the business plan. Because it is a summary, it's best to write this section after all the other topics are complete. The summary is a two-page concise picture of your business. It should be able to stand on its own and cover the main points of all the sections in the business plan. Also included here is your business's mission statement. If seeking start-up funds, most lenders want to read the Executive Summary first before receiving the entire business plan.

Business Description

If your reader has never heard of complementary care, this is the section that will educate them on the industry. This section usually focuses on two issues – national and local industry trends.

Both national and local information should include the following:

- Size of the industry
- Growth rate
- Trends
- Future forecasts

National information can be broad in scope, with the local industry information narrowing in focus. This part of the business description can be as short as 1 or 2 paragraphs.
After describing the industry, your business specifics now come into play.

The information should include the following points:

- ✓ Ownership
- ✓ Legal structure
- ✓ Role in the industry
- ✓ Demand for service
- ✓ Clientele
- ✓ Profitability

Stating how and why your business will be successful is key. This section can be 2 to 3 paragraphs as well. Remember, if you are seeking funding, this section needs to sell the reader on how you can make a profit and why the additional funds are necessary to the success of the business.

Service Description

This section of the business plan should go into more detail on the specific service of the complementary care you intend to provide, by focusing on the benefits of your service. Knowing why someone would pay for your service is a main point.

Here is where you need to explain what separates you from any competition in the area. Using the information, you previously gathered, point out any differences in the following:

- Location
- Hours of operation
- Your training and experience
- Basic pricing

When reviewing your competition, the review should be short and to the point, no more than three to four paragraphs.

Competitive Analysis

In this section of the business plan, defining who your competition is, their strengths and weaknesses, and how you intend to compete with them is the primary goal. Focus on your strengths, services, products, and any other aspect which differs from the competition.

Following are some primary areas to point out:

1. Services not offered
2. Product availability
3. Price differences
4. Location
5. Hours of operation
6. Specific expertise and training
7. Marketing, promotional and advertising campaigns

By listing the strengths and weaknesses of the competition and comparing them to your business, you'll be able to see any potential areas that may need adjusting to assist with the success of your company. For example, if the competition keeps hours on a Saturday, and you weren't originally planning on offering that timeframe, you may want to consider offering it until your client base is established.

Marketing Plan

The marketing plan is one of the most critical sections of the business plan because it requires that you be specific and realistic with the profit potential and growth rate.

Define the following 4 main areas:

1. Target Market
2. Market Size
3. Price Structure
4. Advertising and Publicity

Take, for example, a therapist who wants to focus on Smoking and Weight Loss. The target market would be the number of people in the community that smoke and/or are overweight. A search of the Centers for Disease Control website can yield estimated numbers to start. Once the target market is defined, the next step is to calculate your niche (a specialized market) or market size. This information is now readily available through computer searches. Then describe the price structure of the services and products offered. The final step is to explain the advertising and marketing that will be needed to reach the intended target market. (i.e., When many states started banning smoking on government campuses, restaurants, and other high traffic areas, many health care organizations and hypnotists started offering stop-smoking programs.)

By using specific numbers and realistic goals, you'll be able to see at this stage whether or not your business will be able to turn a profit and have the potential for growth. If the numbers fail to satisfy the income necessary to support the business, redefine, and expand your market. This will save you time and headaches in the long run and give you and a possible lender a more accurate sense of success.

Operations Plan

As a complementary service provider, this section will not be very lengthy, but it's still essential. Here is where you describe how the business will be run.

- Management & Staff – describe positions needed now and for future growth and their job responsibilities
- How customers will be receiving the services provided – individual or group appointments, consultations and seminars
- Equipment – any specialized equipment needed for production or services
- Growth potential – moving to a larger space, renting storage, hiring assistants

Any specialized skills, training, or continuing education also needs to be referenced here as well.

Financial Plan

For lenders, this is the heart of the business plan. The financial plan is your blueprint for success. It takes a little more effort to develop a complete financial picture. Still, this exercise will put on paper whether the business has a chance of being profitable and obtaining future growth.

Estimating an accurate financial section requires completing the business plan. Return to the income projections, balance sheets, cash flow, and funding necessary to start the business when you have a clear picture of costs involved in opening your business.

1. Cash Flow Statement – This is a month by month projection of the money the business will make and the business expenditures. For a very general starting point, take your annual income sales goal and divide it by twelve. Expenses will vary, but consider these items: rent, wages, utilities, insurance, taxes, equipment, supplies, telephone service, consultation fees, and internet access. (See forms page)

2. Income Statement – This isn't as detailed as the cash flow statement but uses the grand totals of that statement, along with any depreciation (equipment, building).

3. Balance Sheets – This statement seems to be the most difficult to construct since it doesn't reflect income and expenses. There are two sections to the Balance Sheet – the assets (items the business owns) and liabilities (what the business owes). These two figures must be equal to each other.

   a) Assets are: Cash in the bank, accounts receivable, property, equipment, real estate

   b) Liabilities are rent, mortgage, equipment, or anything which the business owes money.

These projections should cover approximately three years and show expected revenues and expenses, along with assets and liabilities. Once a basic financial plan is drafted, refer to it periodically throughout the start-up period and the first few months in business to use as a guide. Adjust estimate amounts with actual figures for a better sense of income projections.

Appendix

This section should have back-up documentation of figures, resume of management, lease agreements, contracts, sample marketing material, or any other documentation to show the accuracy of projects and credibility of the industry and staff.

Once completed, it is generally a good idea to have another person read your business plan. Let others help shed light on areas that may not be adequately explained. Remember, if seeking funding, the business plan should take the reader in a logical sequence of who, what, when, why, and how you plan on starting your business. Even if funding isn't the goal of the business plan, remember it is your blueprint to whether or not your business idea is viable and can make a profit.

Blueprints

Writing a business plan takes time, effort, and information. Here are a few ideas to help with creating a winning plan for success.

1. Set aside time to work on your plan – a business plan takes time to create. Don't rush in and expect to finish a business plan in one day.

2. Gather up-to-date information – before writing the plan, visit the library, chamber of commerce, and search the internet for all pertinent information needed. If possible, read another business plan to get a feel for what is required.

3. Know what the purpose of the plan will be – is it to obtain funding or to see whether the idea is viable, or to entice investors? Know the goal before writing.

4. Be open-minded – sometimes, at this stage, changes must be made to achieve a profitable business. Realize that writing a business plan helps you see changes before they occur.

5. Easy access – Put the business plan in a 3-ring binder for easier copying and updating.

6. Make it professional – if others are reading your plan, remember a book is usually judged by its cover. Keep it in line with the image of your business.

For further assistance, the following web sites offer written business plans to read and sample templates for various types of businesses.

Center for Business Planning
www.businessplans.org

SCORE® Counselors
www.score.org/template_gallery.html

Chapter Three - The Roofing

"The man who does not work for the love of work but only for money is not likely to make money nor find much fun in life."

Charles M. Schwab

The best protection a home has from uncertain weather is the roof. For a business, the roof is financing. How much money will your business need at start-up and operate for three to six months? As a business owner, can you continue your financial obligations even if no income is available? How much money do you have available for an initial investment?

What do you have to invest?

The best time to look for funds is before opening for business. The first step is to determine how much money you, as the business owner, have to use as an initial investment. As a service business, less start-up capital is required. Here are a few suggestions for keeping start-up costs low and using what is available to you as a business owner.

1. Furniture and equipment – look around your home and see if there are items that may be used in your office. If you have a home computer, consider moving it to the office since that will be where it's needed most. Look at end tables, chairs, desks. These items can always be replaced or upgraded when income increases.

2. Credit cards – when purchasing items, use a low-interest rate credit card for deferred payments. Consider getting a card with points or cash back rebates for additional benefits.

3. Home equity – many banks are offering attractive low-interest equity lines of credit. Generally, there are two types: lump sum and check-book style lines of credit. Consider which option will be best for your business.

4. Thrift Stores and Discount Warehouses – search for good quality, low-cost items at non-mainstream stores. Buying a case of copy paper is cheaper at a warehouse than at a general supply store. Shop for the best discounts and ask when certain items will go on sale.

Lenders like to know how much the business owner is investing in his company. Make sure to keep track of all the money spent, assets owned, and funds available for your financial statement.

Family & Friends

Borrowing money from friends and family can be either a good venture or a touchy situation. People that know you are sometimes more willing to lend money than a banker looking solely at your business plan. But if you feel borrowing from someone you know will add tension to your relationship, it would probably be wise to seek funds elsewhere.

If you are going to approach your family or friends, keep in mind the following:

- *Keep it business-oriented.* Call them and ask to schedule some time to see them to discuss the proposal.

- *Show them your business plan.* Allow them ample time to read and ask questions about your business.

- *Financial terms.* Know ahead of time how much you will be asking for, the interest rate and repayment length. Have an amortization schedule available.

- *Formalize the agreement.* Put everything in writing to help clarify the terms.

Investors

Because start-up costs and on-going expenses for a service-oriented business are less costly than manufacturing, private investors are a good source for additional funds. Most investors are individuals who are interested in new start-up businesses. A good source for finding an investor is to ask other professionals, attorneys, accountants or through a venture capital meeting.

Investors will want to look at your business plan just like a conventional lender. Unlike a bank, a private investor usually offers cash in stages. For example, instead of a lump sum, an investor may offer a specific dollar amount on a quarterly basis if certain sales are met. And because an investor is taking a personal risk, interest rates are usually higher than a conventional lender. Again, make sure that any agreement is in writing, and have your attorney review any documents prior to signing.

Conventional Loans

If approaching a bank for a loan remember the rule of "C's"

- ✓ Capital – personal investment

- ✓ Collateral – assets available

- ✓ Character – personal experience and reputation

- ✓ Creditworthiness – your current credit score and repayment ability

- ✓ Circumstances – the business and the demand for its services

Your lender will want to review your business plan, see past financial statements, review a credit report, and check any references. Sometimes this process can take a while so don't wait until the last minute to approach the lender.

To save time, start with the bank you currently do business with. Call them to find out the following criteria:

1. Amount of loans – minimum and maximum

2. Usage – what can funds be used for

3. Business loans – Check with Small Business Association

4. Commercial vs. Personal – discuss the advantages and disadvantages of both

Be prepared when meeting with the loan officer. Have all material readily available. Be able to give a 3-5-minute brief on your business and why you need the funds. Remember that banks make their money by lending. Don't be afraid to negotiate rates and terms. And feel free to shop around for the best deal.

Government Money and Grants

As the old saying goes, "there is no free lunch," the same is true with free money. There are many websites offering software and services to secure free government money. Be aware that most grants are offered few and far between with a long and lengthy proposal process.

That said, the Small Business Administration (SBA) is a federal agency designed to assist entrepreneurs with both business advice and financial aid. If approaching the SBA for funding, keep in mind they will want to see all the information that a conventional lender would wish to review: your business plan, financial statements, creditworthiness and character. The SBA will also want to know whether or not you approached any commercial lenders first and what the results were.

The SBA's primary loan program is the 7(a) Loan Guaranty Program – which is when another lender carries the loan, and the SBA guarantees up to 90 percent, making it more attractive to the lender.

The other programs consist of the Low Doc Loan ($100,000 or less), which is less paperwork and can be processed quickly, and the Microloan Program ($25,000 or less), which is supported generally by non-profit organizations and has a short repayment period.

Preparation is essential with both the SBA and the conventional lender. Be ready to answer questions about the business, potential growth, your expertise, owner capital, and other topics explaining why you need funding. The SBA may also require you to attend their business start-up workshop as well.

Blueprints

The number one reason why new businesses fail is due to lack of funding. Make sure you have the money necessary to start and maintain your business before opening your doors. Some questions to ask are:

1. How much money is needed to start the business?

2. What items needed for my business do I already have?

3. What lines of credit do I currently have available?

4. Is there anyone I would approach as an investor?

5. What are the terms of commercial loans offered at my bank?

6. Have I reviewed my credit report for worthiness?

For further financing information, check the following sites:

Business Funding Directory
www.businessfinance.com

All Business Financing
www.allbusiness.com

"Therefore, search and see if there is not someplace where you may invest your humanity."

Albert Schweitzer *French philosopher & physician (1875 - 1965)*

As they say in real estate circles, "location, location, location." That too is the best advice for starting a new business. Your location is an extension of your business and service. People do judge a book by its cover, so keep that in mind when selecting a business location.

Home - Based

Home-based businesses have grown in popularity as well as acceptability by customers. Advantages include saving money on rent, mortgage, and additional insurance, naming a few. A home-based business also saves on travel time, gas, and utility payments.

An office should offer clients easy accessibility for all, including disabled clients or customers, and a level of quiet and comfort.

However, there are possible dangers and inconveniences of seeing clients in a home-based office.

I made an appointment with a home-based hypnotist before opening my Oak Ridge, TN wellness center. The office was difficult to find, and two giant dogs met my car. The hypnotist had to call off the dogs. The dogs later broke through the door to the hypnosis room in the middle of my session. I decided then I would never have a home-based business.

Ask yourself these questions:

1. Is there a separate room or building that can be converted into a quiet and accessible business space?

2. Will noise from children, other family members, or pets be an issue?

3. Does zoning allow for a service-based home office?

4. Will my business be able to grow?

5. Will clients be able to locate my home easily?

6. Do I have adequate parking for clients?

7. Do I feel safe, inviting strangers into my home?

There are also tax advantages to operating a business out of your home. Be sure to check with your accountant for proper home-based business deductions.

Subletting

Another option for saving money during the start-up phase of your business is to sublet—many professionals who own large office space rent out rooms within their buildings to others.

As a business, if you focus on a particular niche within the community, seek out professionals that tie-in with your service.

For example, the following professions usually have large offices and may be willing to rent out a room for your services.

- Dental office
- Physical Therapy
- Oncology Clinic
- Women's Services (OB/GYN)
- Outpatient Clinic
- Acupuncture
- Chiropractic
- Psychology
- Wellness Centers

The benefits to this would be lower rent, a waiting room, conference room, breakroom, and parking available. The downside is that the image of your business will be reflected in the image of the office. If you sublet a room in an established office, you will have little control over changes to the space.

Leasing

When looking at lease space, remember the image you want to convey to your clients. Choose an office building that coincides with the image you want, that is in an area of high visibility.

Leasing space means you have control over the look and feel of your office but not over the building and landscaping. Talk with the other tenants to see how they think about the space. Is the maintenance performed quickly? Is the landscaping kept well? Ask them, "If there was one thing you would change, what would it be?"

Questions to ask when looking at lease space

1. Does this building reflect a professional image?

2. What type of tenant occupies the building?

3. If the space is upstairs, is there an elevator?

4. Is the location easy to find?

5. Is there room to grow?

6. Is there access to the building at night and weekends?

7. What amenities are offered? (bathroom locations, break rooms, waiting area)

8. How is the building zoned?

9. Is there directory signage and a common waiting area?

10. How long has the space been on the market?

11. Request 3 months of free rent to get established before signing a lease.

Ask the landlord for a copy of the lease to read prior to making a commitment. You may want to have your attorney review the lease as well. Talk with your landlord about the length of the lease as well as fixed rent. You may want to keep your commitment to one year, but then there's the possibility that rent will increase when renewing. Know what to expect before signing. And make sure any repairs or other requests are in writing prior to signing. It is highly recommended to have renter's insurance when leasing space. Talk to your insurance agent about different packages and programs available.

Buying

If you are in a position to buy a commercial building for your business, it may be a bit costly upfront, but the long-term benefits are enormous. Know beforehand whether you plan on asking for funds to purchase your building within your business plan. Talk to your lender about combining a mortgage with start-up funds. It's always best to know whether or not you qualify for a loan and the amount before looking for space.

When you have your financing ready, ask yourself the same questions when looking to buy as you would with leasing. Additional things to consider if buying a building are:

- What are the tax advantages of buying?

- Will there be renovation costs involved?

- Is there additional space for subleasing?

- What is the condition of the structure?

- What is the cost of landscape and maintenance?

- Is there space for signage?

- What will the condition be after ten years?

Owning your own business space can be a sign of prestige and credibility. You also gain full control of the design, layout, and image of how your business will be shaped, but the downside is the additional expenses incurred as an owner, such as:

1. Property Insurance
2. Property Taxes
3. Water/Gas/Electric
4. Maintenance / Upkeep
5. Installation of phone/computer lines

> It's best to check with your accountant for all tax ramifications and benefits of ownership.

Real Estate Agents

Whether leasing or buying, you can save a lot of time and effort if you consult a real estate agent. There is a vast difference though between knowing the residential market and the commercial market. Ask for an agent who specializes in commercial property in the area you are interested in looking.

A knowledgeable agent should be able to show you properties that are listed on the MLS, as well as properties that are For Sale by Owner (FSBO's). Before you start your property search, meet with the agent to discuss the following:

1. Who pays for the commission of the sale or lease?
2. Do they charge a transaction or administrative fee?
3. Ask for references of satisfied customers.
4. Ask to see the buildings/lease space they have sold or rented.

Describe to the agent your budget, business needs, and space desires. Sometimes it's handy to have a list of "Must Have's" and "Would Like to Have."

When you schedule a time for looking at property, remember the following:
- ✓ Wear comfortable shoes
- ✓ Bring a notepad
- ✓ Have a measuring tape handy
- ✓ Take a camera
- ✓ Ask for copies of MLS or property info sheets

By using a knowledgeable agent, you can focus your time on what's important, finding the best space and location for your business.

Blueprints

Even if you offer the best service, at the lowest rate, with the friendliest staff, if people can't find you or if the building looks shabby, it could cost you, potential clients. How your business looks and where it's located is extremely important.

Answer the following questions:

1. Have I considered all my options concerning home-based, subletting, leasing, and buying?

2. Do I have a sound idea of my budget for my business space?

3. Will I be able to afford to move if the space isn't big enough?

4. Should I commit to a long-term lease with fixed rent or short-term contract with a possible increase in rent?

5. Have I considered all tax benefits and ramifications of my choice of location?

For additional assistance, check the following websites:

National Association of Realtors
www.realtor.org

National Business Incubation Association
www.nbia.org

"If we are together nothing is impossible. If we are divided all will fail."

- Winston Churchill

When constructing a home, contractors hire subs to assist in the building process. Knowing that a contractor doesn't have the time, money, or experience, subs bring their expertise to the job working as a team for the good of the product.

This also holds true when building a business. As an owner, your time, energy, resources, and experience are limited. If you find it difficult to sub-out or delegate responsibilities, it's time to rethink that strategy.

By surrounding yourself with other professionals who understand your goals and are willing to assist in your success, your business endeavor will have a better chance of growing.

Insurance Agents

Not many people like to discuss insurance. Insurance itself is about destruction, death, or catastrophe; however, as a business owner, insurance is your ace in the hole.

Things to consider:

- Renters Insurance – if leasing space, this will cover damage to your business space and goods.

- Property Insurance – if you own a building, this insurance is usually required by the lender to cover at least the purchase price. Make sure you have enough coverage to handle contents as well.

- Health Insurance – if wanting to expand with employees, benefits are a big draw to the workforce. Talk about joining an insurance co-op with other small business owners.

- Malpractice Insurance – if your complementary care office handles clients from clinics and hospitals, malpractice insurance can help attract more referrals.

- Liability Insurance – this covers any accidents to clients or employees while on the business premises

One way to find an agent is to talk with other business owners. Besides rates, customer service, accessibility, and payment of claims are issues to discuss.

Accountants

Hiring an accountant is sometimes viewed as a double edge sword. Trusting another person with your business finances and monetary decisions or choosing to handle all bookkeeping, taxes, reporting, and financial records yourself. There is a better way.

Consider hiring an accountant as you would a partner. This person should be knowledgeable about your business and goals, have verifiable references, be trustworthy, and have a good reputation. Allow them to set-up the system while you or your bookkeeper track and input the daily records.

 **Setting up an accounting system may seem overwhelming, but consider the following steps:**

1. Buy a software package that can be tailored to your needs – Intuit, Peachtree, QuickBooks, Lotus, Excel, Microsoft Money are programs that are user friendly

2. Know what expenses need to be depreciated and set up an account accordingly – furniture, fixtures, automobiles are just a few items to consider.

3. Billing – if you plan on billing your clients, have a system for tracking accounts receivable, late fees, and past-due interest rates.

4. Employee wages – install a system for paying employee wages, FICA and Social Security withholding and quarterly reports.

5. Tax Reports – tailor your system to track monthly and quarterly income for business taxes.

Some business owners prefer to let their accountant handle all of the finances. This can prove damaging when someone else controls your business's financial decisions. The key is to learn enough about your accounting system and software to be able to do daily tasks. Review all monthly, quarterly, and annual reports with your accountant and have them explain any of the finer points to you.

Attorneys

The best time to consult an attorney is before a problem arises. During the start-up of your business, an attorney can assist with:

- Establishing the business structure
- Filing and recording all necessary business documents
- Reviewing contracts
- Writing and reviewing lease & purchase agreements
- Reviewing and recording financial documents
- Assist in tax planning
- Explaining labor and employment laws

Ask your banker, accountant, or other business owners for recommendations on attorneys—schedule time to meet with them and discuss your business needs and goals. Besides fees and retainers, base your decision on character, professionalism, and business knowledge.

Marketing Rep

As a start-up business, advertising can seem like an expensive wish. Chapter Seven will discuss in detail various marketing approaches. However, if you have the money to spend on an ad campaign, having a marketing rep is priceless.

A marketing rep knows the many aspects of advertising!

- ✓ Direct Marketing
- ✓ Newspaper and Magazine
- ✓ Radio/TV/Billboard
- ✓ Costs vs. Exposure
- ✓ The segment of the population reached
- ✓ Designing, copy, and layout of material

Look at other ads to see what styles and copy attract your attention. Contact those companies to find out who their marketing rep is. Your rep will need to know your business, goals, niche, and target market before being able to plan, produce, and place your ad.

Mentor

There may come a time, either in the start-up phase or while operating, that you'll need to get some good advice. Unless there are people within your circle that are successful entrepreneurs, finding a business advisor or mentor can be difficult.

Sometimes a new business owner develops a relationship with a mentor while training or while researching the business start-up. This person can be an invaluable source for the success of your business.

A mentor or advisor can:

- Identify strengths and weaknesses
- Assist with problem-solving
- Refer and network
- Troubleshoot ideas

Before hiring an outside coach or business consultant, there are many agencies that offer free assistance to new businesses. Know enough about the knowledge and experience your advisor or mentor brings to the table.

- Service Corps of Retired Executives (SCORE) – volunteers who assist new business owners
- Small Business Administration (SBA) – works through universities and colleges
- Small Business Development Centers (SBDC) – scholastic centers that work with the SBA

Blueprints

 Having a knowledgeable team with a defined goal can make your job as a new business owner that much easier. Relying on the experience of other professionals saves time, money, energy, and resources.

Things to remember:

1. Talk with all subs before hiring their services.

2. Look for a person who is knowledgeable about your business.

3. Retain control by having a working knowledge of your accounting system.

4. Know the different types of insurance and what is best for your business.

5. Read all legal documents before signing.

6. Schedule at least monthly meetings with your mentor or advisor.

Visit these websites for more information on Subs

AIG Insurance
www.businessinsurance.com

Accountants World Community
www.accountantsworld.com

Law for Small Businesses
www.smallbusiness.findlaw.com

SCORE ®
www.score.org

Peer Resources
www.mentors.ca

Chapter Six - The Wiring

 "Even in such technical lines as engineering, only 15% of one's financial success is due one's technical knowledge. 85% is due to skill in human engineering, to personality and the ability to lead people."

- Dale Carnegie

With all the equipment that's available for today's business owner, choosing what's best for your company can be a bit overwhelming. During the start-up phase of your business, money can be tight. It may be best to look at the big picture when planning the internal workings of your organization.

Business Equipment

When you plan your budget, set aside funds for equipment needed in the start-up phase, and equipment that is growth oriented.

Necessary equipment can range from:

✓ Furniture
✓ Telephone Systems
✓ Computers
✓ Printers and Copiers
✓ Security Systems
✓ Video Monitoring
✓ Credit Card processing

Telephone Systems

Buying a telephone may seem like an easy task. But think about the big picture. Does the phone have the necessary features that are needed for your business?

Consider the following needs and uses -

1. Multi-line capabilities
2. Voice Mail Boxes
3. Hands-free speaker
4. Do Not Disturb
5. Conference Calling
6. Smart Phone

Check with your local telephone company. Most times they offer a small business package that includes the phone service and computer internet service. Check with the provider in regard to needing a designated fax line or DSL line. Consider where you plan on having desks and your conference room. Make sure these areas have a phone jack or Wi-Fi. You can save money by researching the best fit for your business.

Live answering services are available at reasonable rates.

How a smartphone can make your business

Using a smartphone is becoming one of the best things one can do for business. These devices have revolutionized the way business works. No longer are individuals stuck at desks and cubicles all day and chained to their computers and landlines.

Smartphones give you the option of browsing the web, listening to music, making telephone calls, checking email, taking photos, and watching videos—all in one tiny phone. As you can imagine, smartphones help businesses in many ways.

Here are five benefits that smartphones offer for businesses:

1. **Track and manage your business expenses.** Expensify, BizExpense and are Shoeboxed among the many mobile apps you can use to scan or photograph all those pesky receipts you gather on the road, then archive and organize them in the cloud. It sure makes expense reporting and tax preparation easier than dumping a big pile of receipts out of your bag.

2. **Make presentations.** Tablets are easier to tote along than laptops, making them an excellent tool for impromptu sales presentations to prospective customers. This is especially true if you're in a visually oriented field. With their crisp photo resolution and bright colors, tablets can show off an interior designer, event planner's, or landscaper's portfolio of work to its fullest.

3. **Take customer orders.** Restaurant and bar owners can streamline the sales process by using tablets to have their servers take orders. With less time spent writing down orders and less room for error, your servers can spend more time talking to customers, boosting their tips, and your sales. You can also create fillable forms and have your customers fill them out on a tablet instead of dealing with filling, filing, and inputting paper forms.

4. **Accept payments.** Only 14 percent of small business owners in the survey use mobile devices to accept payments from customers. Tools like Square, Intuit

GoPayment, and PayPal Here are easy to use and enable you to take payments using customer's credit and debit cards, so you no longer have to shut down prospective purchasers who don't have cash. Nor do you have to be a mobile business to benefit—keep lines moving in your retail store (or avoid them altogether) by outfitting salespeople with tablets to make sales on the spot.

5. **Get customer signatures.** Does it ever seem like the most agonizingly slow part of negotiating a contract is getting the actual signature? Speed things up by using digital document signing apps to have customers sign contracts and other paperwork right on your tablet and phone. The faster the contract is signed, the faster you can start working (and the quicker you can get paid).

Computers

As with the phone system, look again at the big picture before buying computers and printers. Ask yourself the following questions:

- How many different types of software will I be using?
- How much memory will be needed?
- Will I have staff that needs a computer?
- Do I need to have a networking system?
- Can multiple computers share one printer?
- Will a laptop be more functional?
- Should my printer serve as a copier, scanner, and fax?

Realize that no matter what system you choose to purchase, most computers need to be upgraded or replaced after five years. When buying a computer system, check on warranties, service, and discounts. If you buy a computer based on price alone and there's no service available, the downtime during repair can cost you more in the long run. Think value not cheap.

Printers that have the capability of scanning, faxing, and copying can save money and space when starting a new business. You can lease or buy a printer that will fit your business needs. The author started with a printer and a separate copier that could only print nine copies at a time. Today, the office leases a combination printer, copier, scanner, stapler, hole punch, and booklet creator. We use all.

List your needs, what you can afford, including the cost of ink before making a purchase or leasing a printer, copier.

Merchant Accounts

Doing business in today's world means being able to accept credit cards. No matter how reasonable you feel your pricing structure is, you will attract more clients if you take the three basic cards, Visa, Master Card, and Discover.

Credit card companies set the rate for all banks. Each bank, in turn, adjusts its fees accordingly. Remember to check with your current bank first before shopping for other suppliers. Besides the discount rate, there are many other factors to consider when choosing a merchant account:

    1. Swipe Rate and Keyed-in Rate – swipe rate is when you have the client's card in hand, Keyed-in is for internet or mail order users.

2. Transaction Fee – usually between .12-.25 cents per transaction.

3. Mid-qualifying, Non-qualifying rate – these are rates for corporate or business accounts and rewards cards.

4. Statement Fee or Account Fee – this is a monthly fee for handling your account, usually between $5-$10.

5. Annual Fee – this fee can range from $25-$65 a month. This is the easiest fee to negotiate.

6. Cancellation Fee – some companies require a two- or three-year contract. If you cancel before the end, they can charge a cancellation fee or lost income fee.

7. Application or Set Up Fee – most companies that charge an application or set-up fee, can apply this to your first month's statement.

8. Charge Back Fee- this is for merchandise returned or disputed items. This fee can range from $10-$50, plus the cost of the item or service.

Most merchant account providers also offer equipment at a discount price if you go through their company. Equipment can be either new or refurbished. Forgo the extra bells and whistles and stick with a machine that has easy dial-up and a two-part receipt. Ask the provider if they have a local representative that will set-up the equipment, be available to train and assist with service problems.

Most companies will ask about your monthly sales and expected charge income. Be realistic, yet know that if estimating too low or too high, the merchants perceive a higher risk and may adjust their rates accordingly.

Above all, ask for a copy of the contract to review. Don't be afraid to ask questions on any terms or rates that are difficult to understand. Weighing the cost of being able to accept credit cards with the possible increase of potential clients is a balancing act. Check with your CPA or accountant for specific financial estimates.

Blueprints

 Whether your office is in your home, leased space, or a new office building, plan ahead for the necessary equipment needed to run and expand your business.

A few questions to ponder:

- Can your clients reach you quickly and easily?
- What type of equipment will your business need to grow?
- How many phone jacks and DSL lines are needed, and where will they be?
- Is a small business package of phone, internet, voice mail, and fax cheaper?
- Will I need a separate copier and fax, or will my printer be enough?
- Have I researched 3 or 4 merchant accounts for their rates and fees?

For further information, check the following sites:

Small Business Computing
www.smallbusinesscomputing.com

Start-Ups Inspiration
www.startups.co.uk

Merchant Warehouse ®
www.merchantwarehouse.com

"Honesty is the best image."
- Tom Wilson, *Ziggy (comic)*

Once the exterior is constructed, the contractor then seeks assistance to design the interior to match the standards of the building. Why spend time, money, and energy in securing the best location, purchasing the most up to date equipment, aligning your professional team, then dropping the ball with a poor image and shoddy marketing material? People do judge a book by its cover, so your professional image, marketing material, and form of advertising need to be selected carefully.

Professional Image

Besides 'dressing for success,' your professional image conveys to your clients a perception of competence, character, and commitment to your profession. A positive professional image needs to build credibility yet maintain your personal authenticity. This means that as a business owner, you need to 'look the part'; however, act in a way that is true to your core beliefs. Otherwise, an inner tension will arise, and your clients and co-workers will feel the tension.

Being aware of your mannerisms, voice, tone, and actions are also a large part of the professional image. Your staff and clients form their opinions by what they see. Theories about your character, competence, and commitment will be based on the total package that is viewed by others.

To assess your professional image, consider the following questions:

1. What character traits do you want your clients to associate with you?

2. What are the core competencies you want to convey?

3. How will you show your professionalism?

4. How do others currently perceive you?

5. Do you care about these perceptions?

6. Which if any of your social identities do you want to incorporate?

7. Which ones do you want to minimize?

As a business owner, you must pay attention to your professional image – to building credibility while maintaining authenticity. Monitor your behavior while noticing your clients and co-workers' perceptions of you. Remember to stay true to your core beliefs and don't be preoccupied with proving your self-worth.

Branding and Logo

> *A brand for a company is like a reputation for a person.*
> Jeff Bezos

In the information age, personal branding is necessary for the success of any company or individual. Failing to manage personal branding can lead to misinformation about you or your company becoming public. Taking control of your public image is no longer an option. Identifying and using the tools that affect personal branding correctly will ensure that the public sees the image that you want them to see. A positive brand is necessary for success.

You are in control of your personal brand if you choose to be. When establishing your brand, it is essential that you define yourself. Remember that perception is reality, so it is essential that you carefully cultivate your image. When you take the time to define yourself and present this definition to the public, you will reap the benefits that come with taking control of your personal branding.

Branding means having a name, logo, slogan or design associated solely with your business. Using your brand in all forms of marketing creates recognition throughout your area and distinguishes you from others in the profession. A brand is unique to your service and business, attributing an image of your company in the mind of your client. The main goal in branding is to have clients know your service simply by its brand. At a glance, the client can recognize your business without having to read any printed material. This is usually achieved by a logo.

In defining yourself, it is helpful to perform a SWOT analysis. By identifying your strengths, weaknesses, opportunities, and threats, you will be able to define your brand and understand what you have to offer. You will also identify areas that need improvement.

- **Strengths**: Strengths are internal characteristics that create a competitive advantage. Accounting skills would be a strength.

- **Weaknesses**: Internal weaknesses that need to be improved. Disorganization would be an example of a weakness.

- **Opportunities**: Opportunities are external. There are always opportunities for you to take advantage in the marketplace. Education would be an example of an opportunity.

- **Threats**: External threats cannot be controlled, but they may be addressed in your opportunities. Competition with a more relevant skillset is a threat.

A SWOT analysis will be unique to each person or business. Taking a moment to honestly assess your situation will allow you to complete a personal SWOT analysis.

A logo is a graphic design with typeset – the company name, initials, or slogan. The colors and typeset or font is part of the logo itself. Its purpose is to avoid confusion in the marketplace among your clients and the general public.

Each organization must manage its brand carefully. A brand is not simply a logo; it is what customers believe about an organization and its products. It is the company's image, which may be for quality, service, or unique merchandise. It takes more than marketing to maintain a brand. Branding requires care at every stage of customer interaction, consistency, and distinctive qualities that set the company apart from its competitors. Once the brand is established, it must be maintained carefully.

A good logo must follow these basic guidelines.

✓ Be unique

✓ Avoid confusion with other logos

✓ Can be reproduced either large or small

✓ Can be printed in full color, black and white, or spot color

✓ Hold its integrity if printed on different material or fabric

✓ Appropriately represents your service and business

Steps:

1. **Determine the Visual Design:** Choose a logo and style for your brand. It may be classic, fun, professional, etc. This style needs to be consistent, so choose something that you believe best represents you.

2. **Determine Your Message:** Each organization has a message that is expressed in its values and principles. This message may be charitable, eco-friendly, etc. This message should be clear to consumers and included in all marketing platforms, including social media.

3. **Be Consistent:** Include the message and design in each media platform. For example, use the same background and logo design on social media and the website. Additionally, no matter what happens, do not deviate from your message to consumers. All communication should support your message.

Social media consistency is crucial and will require careful monitoring, but any inconsistencies that customers perceive will negatively affect your brand.

Choosing a name for your business is the first step in deciding on a logo, and one of the most important. If using your own name, for example, Smith & Associates, a tag line or slogan would be needed to convey your service, i.e., Smith & Associates, Your partners in health care. Brainstorming with others can also lead to finding a suitable business name. If planning on expanding your business, using the word "Center" or "Network" may be appropriate, but not if starting your office from your home.

Once you decide on the business name, check the local, state, and national records is the next step. If your service will be only locally, there's no need to review national or international records.

Now that your business name is chosen, it's time to decide on the graphic, color, and font style. There are many companies that will design your logo for you, but as a new start-up, there are other ways to generate ideas with little or no cost to you.

1. Contact the local High School art department and discuss a competition for the logo with a prize to the top three designs.

2. College or University students in the marketing department can be contacted for their input and design ideas.

3. Post notices in the library and community arts programs.

4. Ask family and friends for their ideas and designs.

If using a slogan, remember it must be short, to the point and convey a message that sums up your service or business ethic. Slogans can be used as 'tag lines' on other materials instead of being tied to your logo. Either way, its message must be clear to the client and convey your service, image or mission statement.

With your business name, logo, and slogan designed, the next step is deciding on the best marketing material to complete your company's branding.

Marketing Material

When starting up a new business, money spent on your marketing is probably the costliest of all items and generally the most important. Remember, once your material is designed, formatted, and saved, reprinting costs are cheaper, and duplicate run ads are discounted. Taking the necessary time in advance to making the right decisions can save money in the long run.

Marketing materials are as varied as businesses themselves. Some materials used in marketing a company are:

• Business cards	• Newsletters
• Letterhead / envelopes	• Magnets
• Brochures	• Calendars
• Post cards	• Thank you, cards,
• Direct Mail	• T-shirts / caps
• Flyers	• Pens
	• Apps

As a new business, the best way to start marketing is to remember who your client is. Business cards are a must-have in any profession, along with stationery. However, if your market niche is women, putting your logo on ball caps may not be an appropriate way to market your company.

Brochures are an effective and cost-efficient way to market. Keerp your information brief, a brochure can define your services, introduce yourself and your credentials, and give the necessary information of location, phone, email, or website. Don't discuss your fees on the brochure. The key is to keep your brochure simple yet give enough information to prompt the client to call for an appointment. Price is irrelevant until a service proves beneficial. Your value determines your fee.

When considering a printer, remember the following:

- Ask for discounts if ordering in quantity
- Write the text to save formatting costs
- Ask to see a proof before printing
- Check if discounts are given for reprints

If you have the software and proper printer, you may want to consider printing your branded stationery, envelopes, and business cards. Keep in mind, however, if you choose to design and print brochures the quality needs to be consistent with the company's image. Sometimes it's best to spend a little more money on an upscale end product rather than using material that isn't up to proper standards. I use vista print for my business cards.

Advertising

As we all know, the best form of advertising is word of mouth. However, as a new business, you'll need to promote your company to start the ball rolling. One of the easiest and cheapest ways to advertise the business is by contacting your local paper for the Grand Opening or ribbon cutting. Sometimes the newspaper will allow you to submit a small article or quote to accompany the photos; if you are a member of the Chamber of Commerce, the Chamber with organizing and promoting a ribbon-cutting for your business.

Advertising consists of one or more of these methods:

- ✓ Newspaper
- ✓ Magazines
- ✓ Billboards
- ✓ Radio
- ✓ Television
- ✓ Facebook
- ✓ Google Adds
- ✓ YouTube
- ✓ Website
- ✓ Email marketing
- ✓ Other social media

When considering print advertising, it usually takes five ads before the general public notices your business. Running one ad may not draw clients. Track all your advertising by asking how they found out about the company. Keep a contact list.

All advertising needs to specific toward your niche or general market area. Check statistics on the internet or contact local ad representatives for information about their readers or listeners.

Radio or local television stations are always looking for interesting ideas. Contact the station and inform them of any free seminars or talks that can be beneficial to their clientele.

Once the business is up and running, the best advertising you can receive is through referrals from your current clients. Ask for an email address to send monthly updates, newsletters, or coupons. Offer discounts or a percent off service price if they refer a new prospect and never forget to send a Thank You card with every referral offered.

Remember, people must know about your business to be able to become customers. Advertising is an excellent way to initially get the word out about the service offered, benefits, and location. Plan on advertising for at least the first two months after opening your office. By using the information gathered about the best form of advertising, concentrate your dollars in that segment monthly.

Word of mouth by satisfied customers is by far your best advertisement.

Blueprints

 Image, branding, and marketing can either make or break a new business. Planning is the key to long term success. Ask yourself the following questions before committing time, money, and effort on advertising:

- Is my image consistent with the company's image?
- Do I dress and act professionally and confidently?
- Does my logo reflect a positive and professional design?
- Are the colors consistent with my business image?
- Are my business cards and stationery of good quality?
- Does my brochure convey a concise description of my services?
- What marketing media reaches the majority of my clients?
- Is my ad eye-catching and to the point?
- Do I have three months of advertising budget set aside?
- What businesses can I contact face to face with my marketing material?

For further research, check out these sites:

Harvard Business
www.hbsp.harvard.edu

Mind Tools for Excellence
www.Mindtools.com

About.Com - Marketing
www.marketing.about.com

Chapter Eight - The Nuts and Bolts

"When employees and employers have a commitment to one another, everyone benefits."

- Donald Trump

The people within the company are what make a business successful. Hiring the proper staff, having a concise paper flow, and sound internal systems for organization are major components of a well-run company. Being prepared at the start-up phase allows you more flexibility and options during the growth stages. Keeping yourself, the staff, and the business organized can be an easy and fun aspect of your job.

The Staff

When it comes to service industries, the staff is one of the main reasons clients will return and refer others to your company. But when, who, and how do you find the right person? The first step is to know when you need help. Here are a few signs that staff may be needed.

- You spend more time on administrative than service work.

- You lose calls while with a client.

- You lose walk-ins while with a client.

- You spend long hours at work doing paperwork.

I consulted with the Small Business Development Center and was told, "I spent more time managing my business than building my business." That was an eye-opener for me.

When potential clients are being lost due to not being available to assist them, it's time to hire. Realize that with the additional income of those previously lost clients, you'll be able to afford appropriate staff.

When hiring, some business owners pick staff then fit a job around that specific person and their abilities. Then they wonder why there is so much confusion and turn-around. Know ahead of time what you need help with by writing a job description.

A job description should cover the following topics:

1. Title of position
2. Supervisor
3. Duties and Responsibilities
4. Abilities and Education needed
5. Days and Hours of job
6. Pay rate

You may find that by looking at your calendar, certain days or times are busier than others so part-time staff would be sufficient.

Once the job description is written, letting people know you are hiring is the next step. There are a number of ways to advertise a position. Depending on the budget and skill level required, here are a few avenues to look into.

✓ Classified Ad
✓ Employment Agency
✓ School Placement Center
✓ Professional Associations

Before hiring a family member or friend, ask yourself if that person truly fits the position with their abilities, education, and training. Sometimes it's challenging to establish a supervisor, employee relationship with someone you already know.

When prospective hires call, schedule an interview. Have an Employment Application available and review it before starting the interview. Set aside one hour for each applicant. And have a few questions ready for the session.

Remember some questions can't be asked, such as:

- How old are you?
- Are you married, single, or divorced?
- What is your religion?
- Have you ever been arrested?
- What does your spouse do?
- Do you have any children?
- Do you own or rent your home?
- Where were you born?

Once you have narrowed down the applicants, verify all information. Call all previous employers, ask for academic records and copies of certificates, and speak with personal references. You may think you can rely on intuition, but it makes better sense to back up your instincts with facts.

On the first day of employment, the staff should complete the following documents:

W-4 Form

I-9 Form

Job Description

Wage Rate

Confidentiality Agreement

Keep these documents along with their application and back-up documents in a locked filing cabinet. After the forms are completed, provide the employee with a job orientation. Give them a tour of the facility, explain the company's service, give copies of marketing material or literature to read, explain any policy or procedures necessary, and reiterate their job description and benefits.

Plan on spending at least one full day with the employee for their on the job training. Have tasks available for them to complete when you are with a client. It's a good idea to have a probationary period of 30 days. This gives you and the employee a chance to see what the job entails as well as if it's a good fit.

Office Forms

As with all businesses, paperwork is a necessary evil. The trick is to use forms that are complete, precise, and don't overlap in the information. Some of the forms required are:

- ✓ In-coming Call Log
- ✓ Visitor Log
- ✓ Supply and Inventory Log
- ✓ New Client Information Form
- ✓ Client Chart
- ✓ Follow-up Visitation Chart
- ✓ Advertising Tracking Form
- ✓ Job Application Form
- ✓ Employee Evaluation Form

The staff can maintain call and visitor logs, supply and inventory logs, and advertising tracking forms. Client forms, once completed, need to be kept in a locking file cabinet.

Have a procedure in place for following-up on any calls and visitors. Follow-ups should be done weekly with the goal of scheduling a consultation and/or appointment. Use a standard letter that can be tailored accordingly for any literature requests. Again, follow up with a call for an appointment.

Policy and Procedures

Keeping good employees and motivating them to succeed, along with your business, can be achieved by letting everyone know what the company's expectations are. Simple and basic written policy and procedures manual is an excellent way to set the standards for what is expected from employees.

The manual needs to contain the following elements:

- Company history
- Mission statement
- Growth goals
- Policies
- Job Procedures/ Position Description

Policies are usually divided into specific sections, such as:

- Dress Code
- Drug Policy
- Holiday, vacation and sick leave
- Benefits provided
- Pay periods and over-time
- Performance reviews
- Grievance process

Procedures for each job responsibility should be written in a concise format that's easy to understand and follow. Usually, copies of forms, letters, and literature are included for easy reference. When writing the procedures, think in terms of training someone for the job. What would they need to know to be successful in their position?

Have your attorney review the manual for any possible discriminatory language and completeness of topics covered. Usually, the manual is given to and signed for by each employee upon the first day at work.

Record Keeping

The three primary records you need access to are employee records, client records, and financial records. All are important and need to be kept private and confidential. As the owner, you have leeway on what files you want to keep and how detailed they will be. The IRS only stipulates that your financial records you identify income, expenses, and deductions.

Staff records should include withholding and payroll tax, unemployment tax, and social security tax. If you provide benefits, insurance, vacation, and holiday records must be maintained as well. It's generally a good idea to give each employee a yearly update of vacation and holiday accrual.

Client records should include all initial information, patient charts, goals and objectives, and professional observations. Any insurance forms or physician referral slips should be on file as well. It's also a good idea to keep a copy of the checks received for payment.

Financial records can be either simple or complex, depending on what system you choose to utilize. Most service industries prefer single-entry records. This is the simplest way to keep up to date information needed. By keeping financial records, you'll be able to:

- Monitor the business's performance
- Make effective financial and management decisions
- Track expenses to budget
- Prepare financial statements
- Compete in the marketplace

Review financial records monthly. Notice actual expenses to estimated budget amounts and revise if necessary. Look for trends, either up or down, in income received. Review all advertising for the most effective modes and ads.

Record keeping removes the guesswork for facts and keeps you in the loop with where your business is heading. By maintaining and analyzing records, you can detect any flaws or favors and act accordingly before they become issues to be faced or opened doors that quickly close.

Quicken or Quickbooks are beneficial tools for keeping track of all the financial aspects of your business.

Blueprints

Having competent staff, concise forms, policy and procedures and record keeping systems in place will allow you to concentrate on growing your business instead of worrying about which way your company is headed.

Answer the following to gauge your preparedness:

1. Am I at the point where I'm losing clients while with clients?
2. Is my time spent on service or administration tasks?
3. What are my busiest days and hours?
4. Do I need full-time or part-time help?
5. Are my forms concise and needed?
6. Are there any forms that overlap information?
7. Is the information kept in a secure location?
8. Is the policy & procedure manual easy to read?
9. Has the manual been reviewed with legal expertise?
10. Is the orientation and training program helpful?
11. Is my record-keeping system organized?

Following are informative sites to review:

Business Management About.com
http://humanresources.about.com

Process Improvement Publishing
www.companymanuals.com

United States Dept. of the Treasury – Internal Revenue Service
www.irs.gov

Chapter Nine - The Landscape

"The service you do for others is the rent you pay for the time you spend on earth."

- Mohammed Ali

When the contractor has completed the building, the final step is laying sod, planting trees, and establishing a yard that will continue to grow and flourish. So, it is with building a successful business. As the business owner, it is up to you to plant the seeds that will allow your company to grow and expand.

Customer Service

With the marketing and advertising that you did, clients will be calling for your services. It is during that initial contact that customer service begins. From the time you say hello to the end of the session, a client is establishing whether or not they will return for another appointment or even refer your services to others.

Make sure that each client:

- Receives a warm and friendly greeting
- Is made to feel comfortable if having to wait
- Listen to them, paraphrase back, and listen again
- Answer all questions and relieve fear
- Call or drop a note to follow-up
- Thank them for their business

Like any therapy, the goal is to assist the client, so they no longer need our service. Therefore, it is imperative to ask each client you see for a referral.

Referrals & Networking

The best form of advertising is the client referral. Instead of you trying to sell your services, a satisfied customer can do that for you. When a client leaves your office, a simple statement of "I'm glad you are happy with our service. Do you know anyone else that may benefit from our service?" Then remain quiet while they think about the people they know.

Another way to ask for a referral is a simple follow-up letter. The goal of the letter is to thank the client for their business, write a statement or two for testimonial use, and list the names and phone numbers of others who they recommend. Once a client has referred a customer to you, call and thank them again.

Sometimes a client is a member of an organization or club. Instead of asking for a referral, ask about their organization and how your services may be beneficial to the group. Smoking cessation or weight loss programs are easily tailored for group presentations.

Approaching other professionals in the community adds to the networking cycle. The first contact should always be a simple introduction with a business card given. State briefly what your services can provide for the benefit of their employees. Offer to follow up with a call to discuss possible presentations. Other professionals may be in a position to refer clients to you directly.

Consider approaching other Professionals for referrals.

- ✓ Attorneys
- ✓ Dentists
- ✓ Physicians
- ✓ Massage Therapists
- ✓ Clergy
- ✓ Family Services

Have a system in place to track who refers clients to you. It is usually a good idea to ask, "how did you hear about us" on the client information form. Always call or send a thank you for every referral.

Promotions

Marketing, advertising, seeking referrals, attending to customer service – all these actions are a form of promotion. However, another way to promote yourself and your business is by offering free services.

Besides these, what other topics fit your area of expertise?

- Smoking & Weight loss with Complementary care

- History of Complementary Care

- Complementary Care methods

- Reduce Stress & Anxiety

- Sports and Complementary Care

- Complementary Care and Pain Management

Many public libraries and local banks offer their conference rooms at inexpensive rates. Consider holding a one-hour seminar for free. Offer basic refreshments afterward so people will linger and visit. This is an easy and cost-effective way to introduce yourself and your business to the community

If planning a seminar, remember the following:

- Have a guest sign-up sheet for the name, address, phone number, and email
- Have plenty of business cards and brochures available
- Make copies of your topic outline for their notes
- Have your calendar available to schedule appointments
- Prepare, then practice, practice, practice

Here are other ways to promote the business within the community.

- Joining the Chamber of Commerce
- Volunteering at local events
- Sponsoring a booth at school events
- Sponsoring an athletic team

Always be on the look-out for ways to get the business name and service known. Be creative and have fun. If meeting others or speaking in front of a crowd intimidates you, consider joining toastmasters.

Creating Products

When paying for a service, the client may feel, "Is that it?" Giving something extra is a way to make the client feel as if they received more than they paid for.

Some products to consider are:

1. CD's

2. USBs or MP3s

3. Workshops

4. Booklets

5. Podcast

6. Blog

The downside to creating products is the time necessary initially to produce the item. However, once the product is created, making copies or reprinting is easy.

If planning on creating CD's, USBs, MP3s, and MP4s. There are numerous software programs that make recording and copying thes formats easy. However, online downloads are trending now. The smartphone and the Cloud have changed how we do business.

Ask your computer tech what system requirements are needed to support software before purchasing. There are free recording software downloads available on the internet, but quality and user-friendliness vary.

Designing self-help workbooks, books, or booklets is another way to offer additional products to your clients. Again, the process is significant on the front end, but once published, it's easier for reprints.

Check with local self-publishing companies for their rates, quality, and marketing assistance. Always ask to see a sample of their books. Most publishers offer price breaks on quantity orders.

There is software available for desktop publishing, and many office supply stores offer binding services. Check all available sources for price, quantity discount rates, and quality.

Copyrights & Trademarks

When spending the time, money, and effort creating a product, protect that product with copyrighting. Copyrights are relatively easy to secure. The U.S. Copyright Office of the Library of Congress has all the necessary information and application on their website. A small fee is required along with a copy of the product you want to copyright. Once the copyright is approved, place the copyright symbol on the product.

If your product has a specific name or symbol, for example, "Hypnobirthing" ®, the trademark can be used. Trademarks protect both the product and service name and any associated symbols for 20 years. Trademarks mean that as the business owner, you 'own' the mark or source of the name or service.

Blueprints

 Growing your business means continually asking for referrals, networking, promoting, and offering tangible products. It's usually a good idea for the first year in business to schedule time weekly for these tasks.

A few things to remember:

- Customer service begins with "hello"
- Treat all clients with respect and confidentiality
- Ask all clients for referrals
- Remember to send a "thank you" follow-up
- Contact other professionals for networking and referrals
- Offer free seminars to the public or organizations
- Consider offering tangible products to your clients

Websites of Interest:

KPD Amazon Free book publishing
https://kdp.amazon.com/

Audacity Recording
http://audacity.sourceforge.net/

Lulu Publishing Company
www.lulu.com

The Library of Congress
www.copyright.gov

The United States Patent and Trade Office
www.uspto.gov

Chapter Ten – Marketing

The aim of marketing is to know and understand the customer so well the product or service fits him and sells itself.

Peter F. Drucker

Thanks to the rise of technology and social media, the world of marketing and advertising has become more prominent than ever. Marketing has gone beyond the classic printed ads, billboards, or even television commercials. Unfortunately, this can cause any company to become confused or even intimidated about getting their product or service out into the market. But if we can learn the right strategies with the right tools, we can break into the marketing world without fear or hesitation.

I find it amazing how web development has changed since I hired a web-designer and got my first website up and running. That website cost more than I made my first year as a nurse anesthetist, and that was a good salary.

All social media, including websites, have evolved so fast and keep growing at such a fantastic pace that I choose to leave this portion of the program to what you already know about building websites through GoDaddy or other web designers. However, social media Facebook, Twitter, Snapchat, and others will let you get business out to the community and the world.

Inform and Educate

Marketing must do more than appeal to emotions. Specific marketing methods need to inform and educate customers. The best way to inform customers and educate people is through your product content. Content is provided through different media:

- Blogs
- Webcast
- Social media
- Newsletters

The content needs to be relevant, engaging, and well written (or well-edited in the case of a webcast). When creating content, it is crucial to focus on one topic at a time, and use subheadings to break up information. This will allow customers to focus on small portions of information at a time.

Facebook

Facebook can be thought of as your little piece of personal real estate on the internet, where you get to customize your profile and make status updates to communicate with your friends. You even get current and personalized news of friends' updates as well as updates from brands, blogs, and public figures delivered to you via the news feed.

Every small business should be on Facebook. With more than 2.27 billion monthly users, small businesses can use Facebook in several ways to promote services and boost recognition.

Using Facebook for business may seem complicated because its rules and algorithms change frequently. However, with the right strategies, Facebook is one of the best tools for targeting a specific audience through paid campaigns. It knows a lot about its users (more so than we ever thought), and it uses this information to your advantage when you purchase ads.

A business page on Facebook gives you a way to communicate directly with your target audience.

Twitter

- Twitter is a 'microblogging' system that allows you to send and receive short posts called tweets. Tweets can be up to 140 characters long and can include links to relevant websites and resources.
- Twitter users follow other users. If you follow someone, you can see their tweets in your twitter 'timeline'. You can choose to follow people and organizations with similar academic and personal interests to you.

- You can create your tweets, or you can retweet information that has been tweeted by others. Retweeting means that information can be shared quickly and efficiently with a large number of people.

Twitter is a short message communication tool that allows you to send out messages (tweets) up to 140 characters long to people who subscribe to you (followers).

Your tweets can include a link to any web content (blog post, website page, PDF document, etc.) or a photograph or video. If a picture is worth a thousand words, adding an image to a tweet expands what you can share to beyond the 140-character limit.

People follow (subscribe) to your Twitter account, and you follow other people. This allows you to read, reply to, and easily share their tweets with your followers (retweet).

How Twitter Is Unique

In the social media world, Twitter falls into the category of microblogging tools because of its short, disconnected messages.

Twitter helps businesses stay connected to their customers and allows the customers to send feedback via their feed. Twitter is extremely popular and helps build brand loyalty, increase sales, and spread and news about the business.

Instagram

Instagram is one of the most popular social media platforms, and every small business should consider using the platform. From gathering insights to selling products, Instagram keeps rolling out tools to help business owners succeed on the photo-sharing social media platform.

It's not too late to join and become successful on Instagram. With the right marketing strategy, businesses can promote products and services, boost their brand, and increase sales on Instagram. Here is everything you need to know about using it to market your business.

Instagram - Similar to Facebook or Twitter, everyone who creates an Instagram account has a profile and a news feed. When you post a photo or video on Instagram, it will be displayed on your profile. Other users who follow you will see your posts on their news feed. Likewise, you'll see posts from other users whom you choose to follow.

Pretty straight forward, right? It's like a simplified version of Facebook, with an emphasis on mobile use and visual sharing. Just like other social networks, you can interact with other users on Instagram by following them, being followed by them, commenting, liking, tagging, and private messaging. You can even save the photos you see on Instagram.

Instagram is a great way to bring people closer to your business by expressing your personality and creativity. And it is not a time-sap. You can set up an account in seconds and draw up an imaginative strategy on a rainy Wednesday afternoon.

Linkedin

With options for job seekers and businesses alike, LinkedIn provides opportunities to find a job, attract top talent, and establish your company as a thought leader in your industry.

And with the rollout of its New Recruiter and Jobs platform this summer, LinkedIn is making it easier than ever for companies to find talented workers.

But you'll need a LinkedIn company page to take advantage. Here's how to create a page and how to best use LinkedIn for your business.

LinkedIn helps you grow and maintain your professional network and is a fantastic tool for this purpose. It's a helpful way to remain in touch with your professional colleagues or even friends. Let's say there's someone with whom you would like to get in touch. Maybe it's a sales prospect, or perhaps it's a hiring manager for a position that interests you. LinkedIn gives you another tool whereby you can learn something about that person, and who you already know that might know him or her. So, LinkedIn provides information.

For the small business owner, a good reason why you should use LinkedIn is to market your business online. A LinkedIn profile alone can earn many contacts and provide a place to display your business contact information and offerings. In addition, you can use targeted marketing techniques to add others to your network who are in your market.

Best Website Builders for Businesses

- Wix
- Square Space
- Site123
- WordPress

Wix

Wix.com is a leading cloud-based development platform with millions of users worldwide. We make it easy for everyone to create a beautiful, professional web presence.

Promote your business, showcase your art, set up an online shop, or just test out new ideas. The Wix website builder has everything you need to create a fully personalized, high-quality free website.

Squarespace

Squarespace empowers millions of people — from individuals and local artists to entrepreneurs shaping the world's most iconic businesses — to share their stories and create an impactful, stylish, and easy-to-manage online presence.

Site123

SITE123 free website builder is here to change everything you have known about website builders.

It is a perfect solution for a private or a corporate Internet user, offering tools that would spare you of any prior design and coding experience and let you handle it without hiring a professional.

The advanced wizard, with its ready-made styles and layouts, will teach you how to make a website and help you set up a perfect online presence with practically no effort.

Upload your quality content, while we are taking care of all the rest, helping you come up with a responsive, search-engine-optimized website, fully adapted to all kinds of devices and screen resolution.

WordPress

WordPress is software designed for everyone, emphasizing accessibility, performance, security, and ease of use. We believe great software should work with minimum set up, so you can focus on sharing your story, product, or services freely. The basic WordPress software is simple and predictable, so you can easily get started. It offers powerful features for growth and success.

We believe in democratizing publishing and the freedoms that come with open source. Supporting this idea is a massive community of people collaborating on and contributing to this project. The WordPress community is welcoming and inclusive. Our contributors' passion drives the success of WordPress, which, in turn, helps you reach your goals.

 Blueprints

Things to remember

It is impossible to communicate with your target audience if you do not use the correct media. For example, overlooking social media for younger customers will almost guarantee that they do not receive your communication. Choosing the right media depends on your customer and your budget.

Types of Media:

- **Radio**: This media only reaches a small group, but you can focus exclusively on your target market.

- **Television**: The media reaches a broader group, but it is expensive, and the message may be ignored with DVRs.

- **Publications**: Reach your target market in specific publications.

- **Internet**: Banner ads and SEO broaden the market.

- **Social media**: Social media allows customers to follow and share, but it requires monitoring and maintenance.

Websites of interest:

https://www.squarespace.com/?channel=pbr&subchannel=bing&ca
mpaign=pbr-dr-bing-us-en-squarespace-general-
bmm&subcampaign=(brand-general_square-
space_bmm)&utm_source=bing&utm_medium=pbr&utm_campaign
=pbr-dr-bing-us-en-squarespace-general-
bmm&utm_term=%2Bsquare%20%2Bspace&msclkid=f3b47b0572c2
19a55fb225d577261c42

https://www.site123.com/about

https://wordpress.org/about/

Closing Thoughts

85% of all business startups fail for many different reasons.

You, the new business owner, read this blueprint discussing the things involved in constructing a business. However, I want to conclude with what, for me, was the key element in my business success, and it came down to knowing what my break-even point was and how much money I would need on hand to cover my business expenses for six months.

The Bottom Line

You are calculating your business break-even point.

1. Calculate your start-up expenses
    a. Loans
    b. Equipment
    c. Other office expenses
2. Calculate your ongoing cost
    a. Phones
    b. Utilities
    c. Salaries
3. List your fixed cost
    a. A cost that has to be paid whether you make money or not
    b. Rent, utilities, phone
4. List cost that may vary
    a. Postage
    b. Paper
    c. Credit card processing fees
    d. Taxes
5. List unexpected cost
    a. Computer failure
    b. Illness as with Covid19

When a business brings in the same amount of money, it spends it is at break-even. When a company crosses the threshold of break-even, it is in the profitability zone.

The first step in profitability is knowing exactly where your business stands on the break-even threshold between loss and profit. You must know where your business's finances are to map the direction to success.

What is your break-even?

How much profit are you prepared to make?

- **Seth Godin**: Don't find customers for your products; find products for your customers.

- **Barbara Corcoran**: Every single thing I learned about marketing and building my business, I learned from my mom, and she had never been in the workforce. She just had practical sense.

- **Nicolas Roeg**: Marketing is an excellent thing, but it shouldn't control everything. It should be the tool, not that which dictates.

- **Joe Pulizzi**: Word-of-Mouth marketing has always been important. Today, it is more important than ever because of the power of the internet.

References

1. Small Business Administration
   a. https://www.sba.gov/sbdc

2. Legal essentials for business | business.gov.au
   a. https://www.business.gov.au/Planning/New...

3. Peer Resources - Famous Mentor Pairings - Business ...
   a. https://mentors.ca/mp_business.html

4. The Business Guides: CPAs and Advisors for Business Owners ...
   a. https://www.thebusinessguides.com/splash

5. https://www.businessnewsdaily.com/7761-facebook-business-guide.html

6. https://www.lifewire.com/twitter-4102609

7. https://www.socialmediaexaminer.com/how-to-use-twitter-for-business-and-marketing/

8. https://esrc.ukri.org/research/impact-toolkit/social-media/twitter/what-is-twitter/

9. https://www.businessnewsdaily.com/7662-instagram-business-guide.html

10. https://www.lifewire.com/what-is-instagram-3486316

11. https://www.businessnewsdaily.com/10376-linkedin-for-business.html

12. https://www.thebalancecareers.com/linkedin-101-the-why-of-linkedin-2062334

13. https://www.wix.com/blog/2010/05/does-your-wix-have-a-title-and-description/

14. https://www.squarespace.com/?channel=pbr&subchannel=bing
&campaign=pbr-dr-bing-us-en-squarespace-general-
bmm&subcampaign=(brand-general_square-
space_bmm)&utm_source=bing&utm_medium=pbr&utm_cam
paign=pbr-dr-bing-us-en-squarespace-general-
bmm&utm_term=%2Bsquare%20%2Bspace&msclkid=f3b47b05
72c219a55fb225d577261c42

15. https://www.site123.com/about

16. https://wordpress.org/about/

Made in the USA
Columbia, SC
29 August 2020